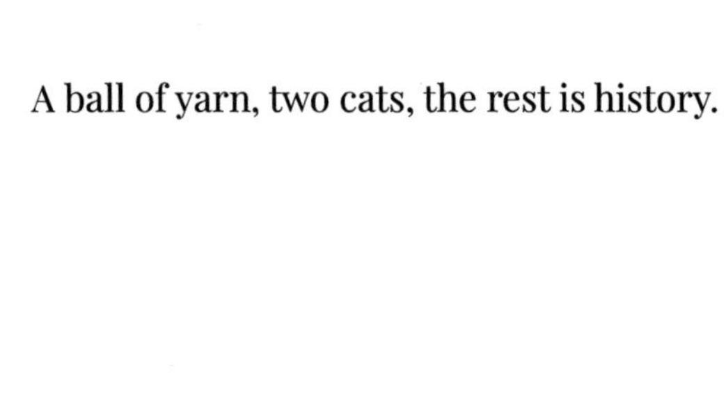

A ball of yarn, two cats, the rest is history.

BRÉMOND

The Sound of Velvet Paws

0°

They met on a dance floor
and went 360 degrees together

in North East London
wherever beats land on.

10°

Among all the foods that start with a C and ends with an E, her favourite is Chocolate whereas he is more into Cheese.

She's a ballerina, he's French.

I just see your msg, can you chat now?

Pas de chat, working on something, but can text, what are you up to?

I am torturing a new pair of pointe shoe

Trying to make them talk?

Breaking the sole and the box of the shoes to make them more comfortable

The box too? Why?

I meant, the hard part of the pointe shoes, which is called the box, it needs to be broken in

You can't make an omelette without breaking eggs

But you can do a pirouette without breaking legs

20°

First date.

Colette says it is not her fault if she is late, she says it is because time disappears in the shower.

I watched some of your ballet tutorial videos

Did you try any of the steps?

If only i had your grace, but hey, i was quite surprised that all these steps kept their French names in English. I would have imagined that ballet companies would use translated terms abroad

True, the French terminology is used worldwide, have you watched any bits of my performances too?

Of course i did

And what did you think?

Well, i don't know how you manage to be standing on one leg, on your toes, with the other leg up above your head and still be able to smile

Hours of training

Impressive

Actually, i watched your videos too

Oh yeah? And?

Well, i think that you should sing more songs in French

But i prefer writing in English

People care more about the music than about lyrics and your image is quite French, it would make more sense as an ensemble i think

Pourquoi pas

30°

Colette, what are these noises i hear on the phone, what are you doing?

Nothing, i'm talking to you

But i can hear funny noises, like you're opening and closing a fridge or something

Oh! You mean that noise?

Yes

I'm doing suctions on my face

Suctions on your face?

It is called facial cupping

I'm confused

Can i ask you a question?

Go ahead

What is it that you are after? Disposable love or sustainable love?

Well, i'd love to share some slices of life with you, what about you?

I'm already in a long term relationship with ballet but i quite like tasty slices

He turned his phone on silent after they hung up and continued walking through the neighbourhood, enjoying solitude, following his inspiration.

Rarely he would feel a need for company as he liked to have space for exploring and shaping thoughts.

However, femininity was meaningful to him. He knew how to attune to his own as he believed that masculinity was taking up too much space in the world.
How feminine Colette was, inspired him so much, but above all, she exuded a type of grace that fascinated him. A grace that was not only smooth, fluid, elegant or effortless, it was also the fruit of a mind that went through many hours of hard work and through tough injuries, which impressed him a lot.

He was ready to learn from her, but not yet ready to admit it to her.

40°

Dance studio.

Colette is warming up, touching her knee with her nose, stretching up one leg on a horizontal barre, doing Pliés with the other, breathing deeply.

Even when it feels a bit tight, being in her body is where she enjoys being the most. Being present in the moment is generally better than being in her head too much.

However, her body is playing with her mind today. She has to focus on the digestion of the beans she had earlier without releasing sound or smell amongst other dancers.

There is an art to holding in silence, like how she's learnt to hide the true pain of crushing your toes in a pointe shoe; the style of Colette is impeccable.

Home studio.

Recording bass, walking fingers on the largest strings, focussing on digging grooves of a 5/4 bar, he is trying to transcribe a smooth feline way of moving into a bass line.

He is imagining a cat strolling across the room with a sinuous, undulating motion.

At this moment, a tiny fly lands on his face, but he cannot use his hands to slap it away.

He shakes his head but the fly persists on titillating his cheek, nose and forehead.

He shakes his head again and misses a couple of notes which transforms his bass line into a simpler version, that somehow seems to sound interesting.

He stops, loops the line captured during the fly attack and finds it rather cool, which, by the conclusion of how it sounds, leads him to wonder if the expression 'pretty fly' comes from a similar story.

50°

Come on, catch up, i don't wanna be walking on my own

You walk fast

You walk slowly

It's part of the South of France package

Come on, catch up

But i won't be able to admire the way you walk with your turned out feet style, i don't always get the chance to walk with someone who tells stories with her legs professionally

Yeah, but for this, i train everyday, my body is used to a certain speed, do you understand?

I do, but what i don't understand is how you manage to be late so often with this super speed?

Perhaps i rely on it too much

Or maybe you're too busy

Busy busy, but never to busy for a bisou, kiss me

Under an oak tree of Hampstead Heath, shoes off, eyes closed, her head on his chest, they're having an afternoon catnap.

A leaf detaches from a branch with a Soubresaut, slowly falls with Pirouettes in Arabesque to land on his forehead, and then with a Glissade, reaches her hair.

In the peacefulness of sleep, they look perfect for each other.

She appreciates his musicality, he admires her gracefulness, they could grow to become a harmonious couple, if only when awake, they could find space for each other outside their personal artistic careers.

60°

Like the weather,
life stroked his neck with a feather.
It tickled, it made him shrug
and slowly enveloped him with a warm hug,
altering his thoughts, generating a profound
feeling about the muse he has found.

The smartness underneath her eyelashes
when her smile flashes
plus the feline
harmony of her line
reflected in his eyes, an image of herself that she loves.
Colette dislikes being alone and he could fit like a glove.

70°

Why are you moving your jaw in such a way?

I am pressing the raspberries against my palate so i don't get seeds stuck in my teeth

You're flattening berries? You're juicing them basically

I mash them against the ceiling of my mouth

And is it pleasant?

It is different, does it annoy you?

I wouldn't say that it is very graceful

It's quicker to juice them than be scraping seeds out of my teeth for the next ten minutes

Fair point, but you look a bit like you're ruminating

That's the thing, i'm more of a grapefruit person, it's a different battle, what about you? What's the fruit you are most familiar with?

Considering what i squeeze everyday in my water, i'm a lemon

A lemon? So we're cousins, nice to hear you're in the citrus family, hello juicy pulp, i'm Grapefruit, enchanté

Lemon, enchantée

The Sound of Velvet Paws

Do you think it is possible to put
something in this bin without having
to stand up from the bench?
With a bit of skills, yeah
But, do you agree with me that the
enclosure makes it tricky
Sure
So why put bins so close to benches if you
have to stand up to reach them? Why not
put them a little further down the path
so the people sitting don't have to smell
them?

I can't smell it, can you?
No, not really
So what's ..
I'm just imagining if it was smelly
Why do you think about something bad if
it's not there?
I'm just questioning the logic of the layout
that's all
How long have you been thinking about
that?
Since i wanted to land a kiss on your lips
and it didn't feel right to do it beside a bin
Sweet
For such a pretty park like Clissold park,
it is not so considerate of lovers is it?
So you see us as lovers?
I feel that we are slowly building a
type of elationship that deserves some
appropriate conditions
Elationship or relationship?
Elationship

80°

Colette is watering her plants, talking to them about her lover, saying that it would be great if he was not so nocturnal or if he could be better at cooking, that she finds it funny to be dating a Frenchman who satisfies himself with tin sardines for dinner.

Until she realises that her class starts in 20 mins.

In 3 mins, she's out of the building.

With her fastest walking speed, she could be at the studio in 18 mins. She could run but a bus would save her from rushing steps.

No red double deckers in sight, she accelerates the pace to the next bus stop.

The road seems to elongate as time is running out, as if the pavements were stretching out to make a point; telling her off for not keeping track of time again.

She needs to breathe more comfortably but more than anything, she needs to learn to leave earlier.

The Sound of Velvet Paws

What have you been up to? You look a bit
dazed
I just had a nap, how was your class?
But you sleep all the time!
It's a wrong impression, because i wake
up late in the morning and nap later in
the day you might think that but i don't
actually sleep that many hours in total,
i'm up most of the night
Are you having naps at night too?
Sometimes yeah, after a good paragraph
or if i don't find the right flow, when i'm
working on the couch, i let my eyelids
drop for a moment
Why not going to bed instead?
Sometimes i do but i don't choose it really,
it's natural, it's my body clock
You live in a different time zone, maybe
you should live on the other side
of the planet
I'm good here, so how was your class?
I didn't get to close my eyes like you do,
well, maybe for a second, when i
sneezed

90°

Please, no

What now?

Either you talk to me or you massage me but don't do both at the same time

Why not?

Because when you talk, you're not completely focused on what you're doing with your hands and i can feel it, a massage is meant to relax me, not the opposite

It is a full moon massage, it involves some reflection

Come on

Remember earlier when you opened up to me and said that it makes you feel anxious to be alone, perhaps you should be happy to receive so much attention right now

I know i'm not easy but if i let someone in my space, there needs to be a harmony with who i am, otherwise...

Otherwise, you get someone else?

Otherwise, i'd rather get anxious

To manage his energy, he is comforting his eyes by contemplating the lava lamp on her shelf.

Luminous lumps, slowly moving, with warm and round shapes, colliding and merging together like ideas, gliding majestically in a liquid and colourful silence, up and down with elastic contours, stretching volumes, splitting into parts and merging again, mixing nonchalance and dignity, playing so easily with the laws of gravity, continuously evolving with infused weightlessness in an odd vertical aquarium.

Absorbed,
he is wondering what sort of music could match this dance, but feels unable to push imagination too deeply,
as it soothes his mind so well
to watch the lava lamp.

100°

Colette takes off her leg warmers, readjusts her tights and leotard, presses play on the stereo and a river of piano notes invades the room, switching the atmosphere into a Baroque era.
She turns on Pointe then goes Glissade, Jeté, Coupé, Pas De Chat, Entrechat Quatre, Soubresaut effortlessly, manifesting the elegance of the allegro.

Holding her core, in complete control of her execution, she is measuring the expression of all her body parts with an athletic and ethereal presence, drawing finest details with the articulation of her fingers as she completes a triple turn.

Colette might often be rushing, doing things last-minute outside the studio but she's always on time with music. She owns the ability to sublime notes and phrases just by moving her body so that anyone gets the finesse of a piece of music while watching her dancing.

If only the estate agency could see it and have the whole picture of Colette perhaps they would be touched by the grace she brings to the society and accept that being late with the rent is part of her personality.
But they won't renew the contract. The competition out there is too hard for anyone who doesn't like to think much about taking care of bills.

If only she could deal with everything in life like she does with music.

Laborious. There isn't an appealing idea coming that could uplift the music piece he is working on. He hits the keys with a random chord out of the tonality to expel his frustration.

His mind is elsewhere, thinking about the offer he made her, to move in and live with him while she finds somewhere else to land her dancing feet.

He realises that the push from his instinct and his willingness to help her would drastically change his solitary lifestyle, and that perhaps, other sides of his personality may not yet be ready for it.

Something intrigues him though. It would be amazing to see Colette everyday and be surrounded by her gracefulness, perhaps she could practise her Pas De Chat at home. He'd be swimming in constant inspiration, maybe he'll get better melodies than the one he is currently struggling with.

He takes his hand off the keyboard, stands up, stretches his lower back, picks up a few grapes from the fruit bowl, goes to his shelf, looks at the picture of the pink panther and pierces the skin of grapes with his fangs.

110°

Colette would like to spend one of her last weekends in the cosiness of her bedroom entirely with him, to see how it works being together for a few days before she takes the decision to move in with him. She enjoys his presence but she has to be careful not to let their relationship evolve towards something more than casual.

Colette's real home is the stage, in the light, wherever that can be. Knowing her career could take her anywhere in the world as soon as her residency in London ends, she doesn't want to feel emotionally attached to anyone.

It is a routine that she is used to, going from one ballet company to another, representing different stories. She knows how to find balance by temporarily rooting in one place at a time and bonding with people transiently.

He is ok with it and the dynamic they found together seems to work so far, albeit perhaps a little complex.

Colette wants to remain free to enjoy her independence but not to the point of spending too much time on her own, whereas he appreciates his solitude and finds it fulfilling being loyal to a muse.

It is Friday afternoon and they're gonna spend a couple of days together, like two cats playing with a ball of yarn called intimacy.

Sunday in bed, purring.

> Do your feet prefer the sensatizon of
> walking barefoot in the grass or in the
> sand?

In the sand, if the sea is splashing on
them from time to time

> And would your fingertips prefer the
> feeling of a smooth piece of wood or of
> some silk?

They like ivory keys

> What about your lips? Would they go for
> the skin of a cherry or of a
> grape?

I would have imagined that after the
weekend we have just spent, you'd know
that it's neither of the two.

120°

He is making space in the living room,
empties shelves in the bathroom,
maybe two more for her creams
and scrubs the bathtub for her daydreams.

Now he's wondering how it is going to be
to live with a morning person on a daily

and how his work is gonna evolve
with him trying not to fall in love.

On Demi-Pointe, Colette rises up
with a Relevé to reach the kitchen cupboard to instal her oats, dried fruits and seeds,
coffee bags, teas, powders and dried seaweeds.

She contemplates the fruit bowl for her lemons,
among his grapefruits, assessing the pros and cons.

Colette feels slightly concerned, it is not going to be easy
for her to resist his cheeses.

130°

That's a lot of tinned fish that you've got
there!

This blue cupboard is like the sea, so it all
depends on the tide really

I've never seen anyone who keeps that
amount of tinned fish before

Have you never lived with a fisherman?

Nope

Me neither

But then what?

Oh no! I forgot that the olive oil was
finished

It's okay, i'm sure it's tasty without it too

But imagine it sliding onto the basil
leaves, invading the slices of tomatoes
and gliding over the cheese

You almost make it sound guilt free

Will you ever stop counting calories?
Olive oil is poetry, it has nothing to do
with calories

What about the cheese?

Indeed, cheese has a lot of calories but it
contains love even more

What made you decide to choose this career? It's very demanding, physically

You see that candle?

Yes

Look at the flame dancing

Beautiful

You could think about the amount of work that has been put in to making such a perfectly straight and tall candle

Sure

But you don't, you mostly see the flame, that's the raison d'être of the candle and there's no point in questioning it. The candle has been created purely for the flame to dance and light up people's faces, it is the same for me, i don't question it

You do light up people's faces

140°

In the bedroom, Colette is putting on a red dress. She is pleased with her reflection in the mirror but the colour might be a little too much for the occasion.

In his bathrobe, he comes out of the bathroom, refreshed and energised by the last shower minute spent under cold water. Enthused by her attractive attire, he improvises a Brazilian accent to show her admiration.

Senhora, i am sent from Brazil dot com, you ordered a hot dance?

> What?

You booked the Gostoso experience, i come to perform it

> Please not now, i don't want to be late to this meeting

Don't you worry about time, at Brazil dot com we take you to a different time zone

> Please not now

But you ordered, i must deliver

> Hang on, let me correct my order, in fact, i wanted a Brazilian coffee

Oh, you ordered a cafezinho?

> Sim

Tudo bem, it's your lucky day, the cafezinho comes with a free Gostoso experience today

The Sound of Velvet Paws

In the kitchen, he is assessing the amount of coffee to put in the moka pot. He raises his voice so she can hear from the bedroom, in his own accent.

Do you want a croissant with it?

Just a coffee, that will be perfect, thank you

Are you sure? A croissant would define you nicely

How come?

You wouldn't be too sweet, you would be rich in layers, hiding your softness inside a strong balanced look

Perhaps a tad too fat too

She comes to the kitchen wearing the red dress.

Oh Senhora, you're looking deliciosa

Incredible the influence this dress has on your accent

150°

I know that you're working, but can i ask you for a favour?

Go ahead

Could you stop slouching?

What do you mean?

Your posture, you should straighten your back

Like this?

Yes, better

Alright,

No, not just for a few seconds, you must keep your back straight, you know, i too appreciate grace around me and seeing you slouching isn't it

Oh excuse me, i didn't know my spine could represent an offence in my working environment, actually, talking of grace, would you mind doing a Pas De Chat for me?

What's with you and Pas De Chat? It's not the first time you've asked

It would inspire me so much to see it

Sorry, i cannot dance ballet in front of you

Why not?

I don't know, it's something i do at the studio or on stage, it'd make me cringe to do it in front of just you

Come on, just once

If you stop slouching, maybe one day

Food's ready!
Oh, i can't come now sorry, i'm onto
something, i can't interrupt it
Seriously?
Yes, sorry, i'm writing something

Why don't you write it later while i'm
asleep like you usually do?

You know, i can't control when the light of
creativity comes on, it doesn't wait for the
night to come out, i'm not a lamppost, i've
got to get it while it's there
So i'm gonna eat alone, am i?
I'm afraid i must keep at it, i know you
have made the effort to cook, sorry
Well, you said you would make the entree

Please forgive me, i'll join you when i can,
i must get it now
It's fine, do your thing, i'm having this
warm

Well, it's okay, i'm coming, it's gone now
What?
The flow
Now don't tell me that i've killed your vibe
It's okay, i had a good bite of it, do you still
want an entree?
Look, i'm already having main now, it's
fine

What about a post-main-entree?
What are you offering?
Artisanal Portuguese tinned sardines
Hmm, go on then

160°

In a warm bath, epsom salts and cedar wood oil,

squares from the reflection of the window are floating on the surface,

water is stroking her nape, making her hair sway.

Colette is in her favourite element, in her body,
delicately massaging her feet

until she lets her limbs rest and opens up her mind to a reverie.

Above her,
vapour is landing on the ceiling,
comparably to her daydreams,

without the need for gravity.

The Sound of Velvet Paws

At the bottom of the bed, a ray of sunlight,

seated, string-gazing, his hands conducting slow Bossa
strokes on the acoustic guitar,

notes detaching like leaves from a tree by a light wind

the warmth of the chords travel over the duvet up in the
air
they voyage to her ears in the tone of autumn.

170°

He feels that she is over indulging on the sound that her cold has created to her voice, that she is exaggerating the sexiness of her tone, prolonging vowels for greater effect, adding long hums between sentences as she is speaking to her friend on the phone.
Now that he focused on it, he can only hear the hums.

She hangs up.

Colette, could you say a line for me please?

Oh did i wake you up? Good morning, what would you wish me to say for you?

Yum, this premium rum tastes of gum,
it's like opium i succumb

Grump, grump, grump, morning grump

On the couch, from left to right.

A yellow cushion, his right elbow. His beard in the palm of his right hand, fingers on his temple.

Above his knees in his left hand, a book set in Brooklyn where a cigar shop keeper shows a writer his collection of photos, saying, *"You'll never get it, if you don't slow down my friend"*.

An Indian fuchsia cushion, her right elbow.

Her right hand holding a comedian's book opened at page 18 saying *"The real difference between man and animal is one thing, pockets".*

Her left leg straight up beside her ear, heel high, toes pointing to the ceiling. Her left hand holding the back of her left thigh.

The openness of a mandarine peel on the hills of an unfolded pastel wool blanket.

In the air, the steam of two teas mixing with the fragrance of vetiver and Ernest Ranglin's surfing notes.

180°

“Come on,
it takes two to tangy”, said the grapefruit to the lemon.

Just them, happy, in this warm picture,
they'll be melancholic about this moment in the future.

190°

You don't really enjoy cooking, do you?

What about my tapenade?

But it's just a spread, it's not really cooking, is it?

Yes, it is

Come on, it's not quite, is it? It's like me saying i'm a fashion designer when i knit a scarf

And what is it then? Molesting olives and garlic cloves? You know there is a lot of history behind my tapenade, i've been making it since i was a kid

Look, they've got some on the menu, shall we order some just to compare?

Why pay for something that we can have better at home?

Mmh i see, so is it why you don't want to go to see ballet with me anymore?

Actually, when are you going to do a Pas De Chat for me?

Should i order us some hummus?

Please don't start

But, come on

Please, leave the waiter alone, we're eating now, we're cool

Seriously, if one has the responsibility of looking after the comfort of customers, one shouldn't ask them if everything is ok when their mouth is full. If the waiter is really caring, he should ask the question when i can reply and not rush me to swallow just to reassure him everything is ok

You are quite sensitive when it comes to eating i noticed

Does it not bother you?

Look, i'm already fighting to avoid calories, i don't need another battle when i'm at the restaurant

200°

He is waiting by the front door of the cinema but doesn't know what film he is gonna watch as Colette invited him earlier as a spontaneous surprise. However, it looks like most films are gonna start soon and she is still not there. He receives a message from her with the tickets. She calls.

Hey sorry, something happened

Let me guess, you were in a bath, got caught by the tide and couldn't swim back to the shore

No, i was baking a sexy cake and the oven turned cold on me

Funny, where are you?

Still at home, there's a great residency that i want to apply for and the deadline is in an hour, so i don't think i'll be able to make it to the cinema, i'm sorry

But you've booked the tickets, you said it was a surprise

I know, but i must send my application before it closes

This can't be real, i left the gathering at the radio to come and join you at the cinema, why didn't you call me to let me know?

I thought i would be finished by then

What a surprise, i should have guessed

The Sound of Velvet Paws

So, how was it?

I didn't go in the end

What? But the tickets...

Well, i figured that it was a better deal to make two people happy than one person half happy, so i gave them to some guys in the queue

What did you do then?

I went to an exhibition about a Japanese artist whose first name rhymes with her family name

And what was her piece about?

It's a book she made that influenced the writing of a famous song about the act of imagining, by a guy from Liverpool she was with, whose name sounds like lemon

Oh, Yoko Ono? What's the book called?

Grapefruit

210°

Please, let's not make a big thing out of it,
i didn't mean what you think i meant

It's not enough

So earlier it was too much and now it's
not enough, what exactly do you want?

I want you to show me that you don't hold
grudges against me

But if i did, i wouldn't welcome you in my
heart like i do

Well, nice of you to welcome me in it, but
is it tidy enough for you to have me in
there?

Tidy enough? But what do you mean?

Maybe you should think about it

My heart goes broom for you

Playing with words might be useful as an
escape but they don't solve problems you
know

Late at night, he is typing away, working to make some lines sound less clunky, fighting against his French way of making sentences to improve his flow in English.

She is asleep but her question comes back hitting his mind. The more he thinks about it, the more he thinks about it.

Maybe she felt something.
Something deeper than just him trying to preserve his heart from opening to her.
Maybe she felt that some of his old troubles are still present in him, influencing his ability in dealing with feelings.
Maybe she sees something that he can't comprehend.

How does one tidy his heart? How does one resolve the past? How far back should one look?

He takes a notebook and writes,
When i was in an egg,

then realises he wrote that same line in his first book already. He drops the pen and goes to the kitchen to make himself an omelette.

220°

In the living room, Colette is quietly spreading her limbs on her yoga mat, mindfully focused on her body, attune to her breath and inner world, feeling her muscles.

A fillet of smoke is escaping from the stick of incense on the side, creating ethereal shapes.

With supple slowness, she gets on all fours, grounds into her breath whilst curving her back, swinging her imaginary tail, then reclines into to a child pose.

She wants a long restorative yoga session to release the unpleasant vibes occupying her mood. She wants to dive in, quiet her mind down and reduce the chatter about her cycle being so late.

Within the narrowness of the rectangular mat, she withdraws inside to find space to comfort herself.

The negative pregnancy test was not enough of a relief for her mood like he hoped. He didn't even dare imagine how complicated it would have been if it turned out to be positive.

He is not sure what to do. He goes to put on music, thinking an upbeat track could reignite her happiness, or his at least.

He presses play and unleashes a colourful beat in the speakers that should invite any dancer to feel a stimulation around the shoulders or the neck.

After a few bars, he still can't witness any positive reactions from Colette, perhaps the volume of the music created the opposite, now he is dancing on eggshells.

He sings to expel some energy stuck in his frustration, *"Why is it so difficult? Why is it problematic? Have you checked your horoscope? Tell me what does it say, is today just a no-go? Any possibility to get a miracle?"*

She remains silent in her yoga position, with her mat like a boat the sea takes away from his coast.

He fades out the tune and goes writing instead.
Better to create a cat strophe than a catastrophe.

230°

Colette is cracking all the joints of her feet, her moon has finally arrived. Her energy is low, she'd love some quiet time alone, or being wrapped in warm and soft attention. She definitely needs some calm to be in the process of her cycle.

Would you care for a nap?

A nap where you and i merge into a dream?

That would be great

What would you like to dream about?

About you and me being quiet and relaxed without any kind of disturbance

Basically, you want a dream set in a desert

Could do

Shall we get a camel?

Just a palm tree would do

The Sound of Velvet Paws

On the couch, from left to right.

The Indian fuchsia cushion, his head.

Her head on his chest, a ray of sun on her hair.

The pastel blanket spread over their bodies.

A new teal cushion, her feet, ankle and calves in long blue socks. His feet in green socks.

The yellow cushion.

In the air, Bill Evan's notes mixed with the fragrance of patchouli.

240°

He is trying to avoid moaning
but it is the morning
and he finds the music at the vintage shop
a bit too sweet like lolly Pop.

She tries on a blue tutu
but likes the red one too,
it comes to sit
like an umbrella above her feet.

250°

What are you cooking?
A gustative voyage to the South of France
Wow, what is it?
A celebration of mother nature, a poetry of Mediterranean flavours
How's it called?
A parmigiatouille
I've never heard of it
No one ever did, i am inventing it now before your eyes
What's in it?
Courgettes, tomatoes, peppers, onions, aubergine, garlic, basil, herbs de Provence, olives, olive oil and layers of cheeses

I like it when you're inspired with food

A windstorm of black pepper followed by a rain of sea crystals and hop in the oven for 20 mins

Will you make love to me like you make a parmigiatouille?

I must warn you that my mouth had a fair amount of garlic during the chopping process

I want you to garlic me all over

The Sound of Velvet Paws

So how do you find the parmigiatouille?
I don't mean to mousse you but it's delicious

And how healthy it is!
Yeah, but the chee..

No. Don't give me your 'yeah but', there is nothing i can hear that follows a 'yeah but'
Don't hiss at me, it's just a figure of speech

'Yeah but' is a sanitiser that eradicates the necessary germs for the growth of any good ideas
That much?

'Yeah but' is a crime against creativity, it's the..

So how would you say it then?
'What about'
'What about'?

'What about' doesn't disregard what has just been said, whereas 'yeah but' stifles any form of life that it lands on

'What about' you chill out a little bit

Ah voilà, much better, thank you

260°

Colette is doodling, dawdling, peacefully sitting at his desk with her feet on each side of the chair and pointing opposite directions.

She puts the pen down, raises her arms to stretch her back and shoulders with a little wave of her upper body.

In a continuous motion, she brings her legs back together, lays her palms on her thighs and pushes the chair back with her derrière while pressing her feet on the floor.

She stands up and does a little hip hop, just to readjust bones and molecules. She steps towards his guitar, picks it up and puts the strap on like she wants to satisfy a sudden rush of curiosity, without knowing how to play the instrument.

Like someone checks the temperature of a pool with a toe, she strokes the strings with her thumb tentatively and generates a few notes. She tries again with little motivation to improve, anyway, she's not too bothered if it doesn't sound good after all.

Because above all, Colette is procrastinating and anything is more inspiring than what she had planned to do.

Olle!

Oh wow, what was that?

It's called a Débridé

a Débridé?

You can follow it up with an Effréné, it's an avant-garde ballet step, don't you know it?

I've never seen such a combination of moves before

Well, of course it is a bit more modern than a Developé or a Chassé, i can teach you, but i'll have to charge

Sure, how do you do?

Well, the secret is to start with a little Déchaîné like this, which is quite different to a Pas De Deux as the man, with one hand on the woman's hip, grabs her back thigh with the other, like this, lifts it with control, and as her chin remains up, he comes threatening her neck with his fangs while her claws release as if to sink into the skin of his back

Hmm, could this avant-garde ballet step have some sort of Tango influence?

Absolument

You just ripped my dress

It's part of the choreography

Hmm

270°

Why don't you sit instead of eating out of the cupboard standing?

It's just a quick nibble, i'm working on something, i don't want to settle for too long

Remember what you said about people who eat chicken out of a bucket?

Come on Colette, that's completely different, i just don't want to lose my flow

Yeah, but you should be conscious of what you're doing, especially when you're eating

Sure

Did you know that when you eat standing up, you eat faster?

That was the point, yeah

Yeah, but your stomach moves food faster down your digestive tract which also makes you swallow more air, which leads to some gas

Ah right! And i was blaming cabbage earlier

It seemed hazardous at first, but he managed to impose upon Colette his need to go on a solitary evening walk without creating too much tension.

He is strolling on wet pavements, around corners, street after street, like turning pages of an urban book. A new decor unfolds each time with imaginable stories from the lit windows of houses along the roads.

He is thinking about the audition she went to earlier, because if she gets the part, she will have to leave London and move abroad.

Maybe that's what it is, he feels, and that's the path of her destiny and how their story should end.

The thought grows to create a quiet sound resonating in the cave of his heart, with a soft minor tone, carrying an emotion, slowing down his walk.

A shadow of love lands on his breath, softening his energy until he enters the corner shop.

280°

Quietly in the bathroom, post evening bath and with pores open, hair wrapped in a towel, she's applying cream on her feet with awareness like she knows every nerve of her toes.

Colette has cream for every part of her body, cream for every time of the day, cream for every type of weather, creams, creams, creams, as a compensation for all the ice creams that she doesn't allow herself to have.

She is envisioning herself being part of the ballet company she auditioned for and works to manifest a positive outcome by projecting optimistic thoughts and vibrations.

Out of this vortex of energy, with an active brush of her teeth, she spits out toothpaste in the bathroom sink. Refreshed by spearmint in her breath, she feels a sudden urge to reconnect with him deeply.

The importance of the present moment hits her, that's all there is, she tells herself.

There is nothing more that he should add to that piece, but he's got the guitar in his hands and the full moon is kicking.

Colette silently slinks behind his chair, puts her hands on his shoulders then slides them down into his shirt to reach his chest hair. Her mouth gets closer to his left ear and she hums notes in the tonality of the song. He shivers but keeps on playing the chords like nothing is happening.

She raises in Demi Pointe, goes around him with one and a half a Chaîné turn, lifts the towel tied up around her chest so she can sit on his lap, knees widely apart, leaving enough space not to alter the flow of his hands on the strings.

She unties the towel from her head and, with a quick shake, whips the air with wet strands of hair. With a short blow she removes stray tendrils from her lips.

She stretches out her arms, slides her hands on his beard and above his ears, running her fingers through his curls.

They are sandwiching the guitar. The chords open, filling the confined space between the two human buns with a Bluesy dressing.

She French kisses him, bites his neck, exhales hot air into his ear to express silent notes of desire.

290°

It is 4.45 am, he swiftly slides in bed like a ninja trying to not wake her up.

He manages to lay down without shaking the mattress too much nor bumping against her in the dark.

Now he's got to reconquer his legitimate part of the duvet trapped under her sleeping body.

He gets closer, slowly grabs her thigh and lifts it to pull some duvet over to him, she breathes louder, he stops.

The corner he managed to get is just enough to cover his belly.

He tries to pull some more but the duvet is stuck under her other leg, maybe he should just forget about it.

She suddenly takes a deep breath, turns to envelop him with the heat accumulated in her sleep, covers him with softness and warmth like she was cashmere.

Since Colette received the good news about the audition, heir couple bubble floats in limbo. He is happy for her and she is over the moon.

The feelings that have grown between them are like lowers standing in the morning, with petals that an mpending storm forces to close early as the sky darkens.

t is now the matter to finish what they started, like two dancers end a Pas De Deux, with strength and as much grace as they can possibly show.

But not just yet perhaps.

t is Monday, nearly midday and they're still in bed. They et the week start without them.

They'll catch up later, or find a shortcut.

300°

Tinned sardines
for din dins,
he is thinking to say something
but instead he starts to sing
as his quickest exit
is not always wit.

She finds it hard to re-bond
and rebound,
since she's been chosen for the part
her mind and her heart
are quiet like a firework,
with her emotions propelled like a champagne cork.

310°

Hey! What are you doing here?!

I came to watch you practising

You could have asked

You would have said no

That's right, how long have you been here for?

Well, not long enough

You cannot stay here

I didn't come alone

What?

Check this out

Tinned sardines?

Somehow, this sunny weather inspired me to celebrate your new job and create delicious memories before you get swallowed up by the insular world of this ballet company

So you brought some sardines

The best tin of my collection, have you got a break soon?

Absolutely

Unfortunately, i didn't get to see you do any Pas De Chat earlier

The part i am working on today doesn't include any

Don't get me wrong, it was fantastic to see you move

Thank you

So, i will never get the chance to see you do one for me

Aww, i'm sorry, i've told you, i can do it professionally but i find it too difficult to do it privately, it is hard to explain

That's ok, i understand

I don't see what's so special about seeing me doing a Pas De Chat, is it a fetish or something?

A Pas De Chat expresses so much grace, when the legs form the shape of a diamond, it gives me the impression that the divine is talking to me

That much?

I'm just gathering elements for a future piece

What sort of piece?

A book

A book about ballet?

A book about cats

320°

Colette just noticed her passport is out of date, a rush o panic hits her. Back and forth, in circles, like when a ca has the zoomies, she runs in her mind to find a solution looking at all possible and impossible options to get a nev one rapidly, until she realises, when looking again, tha she confused issue with expiry date.

The pressure vanishes, a deep sigh of relief blows out th fire of stress, all good.

He opens the window for some fresh air, starts singing, and now like a French accordion, he breathes out melodies.

330°

Why don't you say anything instead o moping around? All i hear is the sound o velvet paws

Smoothness is soothing

Express yourself, don't sweep it unde the rug again

It's fine

You have swept too much stuff unde your rug

It's alright, it's a comfy rug, it's got pretty nice colours, why do you care about what's under it?

Because you don't realise that this rug this comfy rug like you say, is a magi carpet. And you won't be able to fly if yo keep hiding things with it

You'd get dust in your eyes if i start shaking it

Would i?

We talked about it, we know that a long distance thing won't work for us

Unless you fly to me with your magic rug

You'd like me to come to the window of your dressing room during shows while you're waiting for your cue?

Actually, too risky, you'd mess with m make up

It is a pitch black night, the moon is either new or hidden. The weather is drizzling, London style.

Telling by the people singing, there is a birthday party going tonight among the neighbours. The building is vibrating from the deflagration of the sound system. The loud bass repeats itself but doesn't seem to wake up the ballerina somehow.

The ball of the pen is rolling on the paper. Trying not to think about his muse, he is writing about London, quite happy with the acronym he just found.

Lots Of Noise Day Or Night.

He leaves his desk, lights a candle and carries it to the bedroom. He sits on the bed next to her and passes his hand on the back of her head. His strokes on her hair are soft as if to transmit the emotion of gratitude and admiration that has been filling him up all evening and that he couldn't express with words. She sighs a welcoming sound.

He slides his paw along her lines.
Colette harmonises his spontaneity by angling her hips.
He puts the candle down on the side to let his fingers go on a night walk.

Outside, the rain has grown stronger and is hitting the windows. Downstairs, the bass keeps booming on the ceiling, vibrating the floor. The future ex-lovers follow their own tempo.

340°

Colette steps on the scale and looks at it with disappointment. It says she has put on some weight. Perhaps her heavy heart is influencing the numbers.

The forthcoming end of their relationship isn't easy for her but she knows it will pass. So many times she's learned to deal with pain when training or dancing, she knows what to do.

She's got to hold her core and position while her partner carries her until the conclusion of the detachment, so the motion of the moment looks timeless and weightless.

A shadow of love lands on her breath, softening her energy until she enters the warm water of the bath.

The record vinyl is spinning, the needle is in the groove, the mixer is on, the speakers are plugged but the song is interrupted by silences.
There must be something wrong with the wires.
He angles the cable, trying to improve the connection.

The song is ending, he is waiting for the next one and still, nothing comes out of the speakers.

He wonders if the silence is created by the sound system or if the next song hasn't started yet. He looks at the situation as an analogy of his relationship with Colette.

350°

It is dawn, Colette wakes up realising with a sudden panic that she is alone in bed. She sits up abruptly and hears him in the living room, still working, on a new song apparently.

She silently listens to his quiet singing. The door muffles the sound but she can hear enough lines.

"If life's just passing like a cloud and vanishes,
moments with you will always remain like a ray of sun in my soul

I know you're here to shine a light, that's what you do,
i'm grateful to have deeply felt it,
maybe that's what we call love

And if you'd hear me singing now, that's what i do,
i throw these emotions in the sky and let them go with the wind

May it blow on them so you can feel the truth,
the meaning of my whole existence
maybe that's what we call love"

She lays on her back, envelops herself with the duvet then turns to her side.
Warm tears are rolling on her smile.
She forces herself to fall back to sleep.
She wants to wake up again with him in bed as if nothing happened, as if she dreamt it all.

The Sound of Velvet Paws

On the couch, from left to right.

The folds of the pastel blanket.

The teal cushion stained with berries.

The yellow cushion.

A book open to a line that says, *"Animals are inspirational. They don't know how to lie. They are natural forces."*

A blue jumper.

The Indian fuchsia cushion.

In the air, the smell of a banana peel mixed with Wes Montgomery's sliding notes.

360°

To uplift the end of the story
he lays his hands on the keys to build a last memory,
improvises a medium allegro in 3/4,
some style he never played to her before
just to see how a surprise
could spark in the universe of her eyes.

From fifth position into a Demi Plié
she springs sideways,
holds suspension in the air,
big toes touching in a quick affair
so that her legs form a diamond
just to say, that one's for you Brémond.

Fin de la Pirouette.

The Sound of Velvet Paws

First edit by Mathieu Cuenant
Final edit by Simone Sylvester
Hand-painted cover by Jack Hewitt
Book design by Elphège Barthe

ISBN: 978-1-9163578-8-4

2024 - 1st edition of 300 copies
Bremondsboutique.com